COOL KIDS COOKBOOK

Hodder Moa

National Library of New Zealand Cataloguing-in-Publication Data
Cool kids cookbook / Top Shelf Productions.
TV tie-in.
Includes index.
ISBN 978-1-86971-109-2
1. Cookery—Juvenile literature. [1. Cookery.] I. Top Shelf
Productions. II. Title. III. Cool kids cooking (Television program)
641.5123—dc 22

A Hodder Moa Book
Published in 2007 by Hachette Livre NZ Ltd
4 Whetu Place, Mairangi Bay
Auckland, New Zealand

Concept developed by Top Shelf Productions Ltd
Illustrations by Muk Puddy Animation
Designed and produced by Hachette Livre NZ Ltd
Printed by Tien Wah Press Ltd, Malaysia

CONTENTS

CONTENTS
CONTINUED

SWEET THINGS

THIRST QUENCHERS

ACKNOWLEDGEMENTS

Top Shelf Productions would like to thank the following people for their invaluable contribution to *Cool Kids Cookbook*: Director Celia Offwood, Producer Brian Holland, Executive Producers Laurie Clarke and Vincent Burke, Production Manager Juanita Dobson, Researcher Georgia Burn, Recipe Coordinator Pam Jenkinson, Recipe Coordinator Jacqui Freeman, Production Assistant Briar Burbush, and also to Andy Jacquet and the TVNZ team.

A special thank you to Kerry Price of the Auckland Regional Public Health Service and Marco Kouch, who came up with the Cool Kids Cooking concept.

Thanks also go to publishers Hachette Livre NZ Ltd, especially to project coordinators Jane Hingston and Caroline List, and designer Craig Violich.

Thank you to Muk Puddy Animation who designed the CKC logo and the cartoon characters which appear in both the book and television programmes.

A big thank you to the following schools for giving their time and resources to make *Cool Kids Cookbook* a success: Birkenhead Primary, Kristin School, Nga Iwi Primary, Onehunga Primary, Oratia District School, and Parnell Primary.

Special thanks to the CKC sponsors, without whom the project would not have been possible: 5+ A Day, Auckland Regional Public Health Service, House Of Knives, NZ Beef & Lamb, and Pams.

INTRODUCTION

At last — *Cool Kids Cookbook*, the book from the acclaimed TV series, 'Cool Kids Cooking'!

Just for kids, *Cool Kids Cookbook* is unique. It is designed to inspire kids to put junk food aside, jump into the kitchen and get creative.

The 'Cool Kids Cooking' TV series, from which this book is derived, is a fresh, fast-paced cooking show. In each episode, talented chef TK, assisted by the comical 'Head Chef', demonstrates basic kitchen skills, cooking tricks and tips as they and their young guest cooks create super-healthy, super-tasty meals that are quick to prepare and easy to make.

Typical recipes include popular favourites such as French Toast, Spaghetti Bolognese, Chop Suey, Fish Fingers, and even Pizza and Hamburgers! There is also a great range of yummy drinks, snacks and dessert treats.

All dishes are designed to be healthy, full of flavour and most of all . . . fun to cook! The team has worked closely with Auckland District Health Board dieticians and the 5+ A Day team to ensure that all the recipes in this book and on the show are packed with goodness. 'Cool Kids Cooking', and now *Cool Kids Cookbook*, will motivate children to choose nutritious meals they can eat at home and take to school.

Although the recipes in *Cool Kids Cookbook* can easily be prepared and made by children, adult supervision is recommended for any recipes requiring cutting, grating or cooking on the stove and in the oven.

TK, Head Chef, Jaz and the team at Top Shelf Productions

WHAT DOES THIS MEAN?

ABSORBENT

Something that is able to soak up water easily, such as absorbent paper kitchen towel.

AL DENTE

To cook pasta until it is soft on the outside, but still a little firm when you bite into it.

BAKE

To cook in an oven preheated to the temperature it says in the recipe. Most ovens have three racks. Position the rack BEFORE you turn on the oven.

BATTER

A mixture of flour and other things like baking powder, salt and sugar to which you add liquids, such as milk, and usually eggs. Many recipes show you how to make a batter by combining 'wet' ingredients with the dry ones.

BEAT

To mix two or more ingredients together vigorously with a spoon, fork or an egg beater using a circular motion until the mixture is smooth and has no lumps.

BLEND

To mix ingredients together until very well combined. This is usually done in a blender.

Boil

To cook a liquid in a pot on the stovetop until bubbles rise in a steady pattern and break on the surface of the liquid. You will see steam when a liquid is boiling. Be very careful as boiling liquid can cause serious burns. Always keep pot handles turned away from you and use the back burner of the stovetop for boiling. Use oven mitts or gloves to handle hot pots.

Break an Egg

Experienced chefs crack eggs by gently tapping the egg on the side of a bowl to crack the shell. Place the tips of your thumbs inside the crack and open the shell.

Chill

To refrigerate something until it is completely cold throughout.

Chop

To cut food into small pieces. Do this very carefully with a sharp knife on a cutting board, never on a counter top or a plate. If the recipe asks you to finely chop an ingredient it means for you to chop it into very small pieces.

Core

To cut out the stem and remove the seeds from fruits such as apples.

WHAT DOES THIS MEAN?
CONTINUED

DICE
To cut food into small and even 0.5 centimetre cube-shaped pieces.

DRAIN
To strain away liquid (like water or grease you don't need anymore) using a colander or sieve. Always drain over the sink. If the pot you are draining is heavy ask for help! Drain grease into a metal can. Do not pour grease down the drainpipe because it can clog up the plumbing.

DRIZZLE
To dribble drops of glaze or icing, or other liquid such as oil, over food from a fork or a spoon. Drizzling thin icing (which is a glaze) onto a cake using a zigzag pattern makes it look really cool.

FOLD
To mix gently using a spatula by cutting through batter in the centre and lifting up towards the edge of a bowl. Use a down, up and over movement, turning the bowl as you go. Be gentle!

GARNISH
To add little bits of something tasty or colourful, such as parsley or other herbs or grated cheese, to the finished dish to add some extra flavour or colour to it.

GREASE

Greasing a baking dish makes it easier for the food to come out once it is cooked. It also makes for easier clean up (a bonus if you are doing the dishes). To grease a dish, rub the inside bottom and sides with butter, margarine or cooking oil. The easiest way to grease a pan is to spray it with non-stick coating, but be careful to spray away from yourself and do not inhale the fumes.

GREASE AND FLOUR

Sometimes recipes will ask you to do this. Grease the pan or tin first and then very lightly sprinkle a little flour on top and tap and tilt the pan so that the flour coats all the insides evenly.

KNEAD

To work dough (like bread dough) into a smooth, elastic-feeling mass by curving your fingers and folding the dough towards you and then pushing it away using the heels of your hands. Do this in a quick rocking motion several times over.

LET STAND

This means to let baked food cool down slightly on a wire rack while it is still in the pan you baked it in. Sometimes food needs this extra time to keep cooking and to 'settle'.

LUKEWARM

Only just warm to touch.

MARINADE

The seasoned liquid you use to soak or 'marinate' food in before cooking (see below).

MARINATE

To soak food, usually meat or fish, in a mixture of ingredients (a marinade) before cooking or serving to give it extra flavour. It also helps make meat more tender.

MASH

To squash cooked or very ripe foods with a fork or potato masher.

MELT

To heat a solid food (like butter or margarine, cheese or chocolate) until it turns into a liquid. This is often best done in the microwave. Melted foods can burn quickly, so be careful.

MIX JUST UNTIL MOIST

This means combining wet and dry ingredients until the dry ingredients are slightly wet or damp. The mixture will be lumpy and that's okay. Some batters, like muffin batter, will not bake well if they are over-mixed.

OPTIONAL

An ingredient you can choose to use if you want, or if it is available.

PEEL

To cut the skin off of a fruit or vegetable using a peeler or a sharp knife.

PROVE

To let a yeast dough stand in a warm place to double in size.

ROUNDED TEASPOON (OR TABLESPOON)

A rounded teaspoon of salt would have a little extra salt mounded up (heaped slightly) on top. In the old days, it meant 'adding a touch more'!

SAVOURY

Food which is salty or spicy rather than sweet.

SHRED

To cut food finely into thin narrow strips.

SIEVE

To strain liquid through a sieve or strainer to separate out the solids. This is similar to sifting, but not quite the same. To sift is to pass dry ingredients, such as flour and icing sugar, through a sifter to remove any lumps.

SIMMER

To lightly cook a liquid (soup, stew, broth or sauce) in a pot over very low heat on the stovetop so that slow bubbles appear on the surface around the sides of the liquid. This is different to boiling when bubbles break quickly on the surface and lots of steam appears.

SKIM

To remove fat or scum (which often forms when you have brought a liquid to the boil quickly) from the top of the liquid using a large spoon.

STERILISE

To clean something using boiling water to kill harmful bacteria (germs).

SUBSTITUTE

To use one ingredient to replace another, such as using prepared crushed garlic from a jar instead of freshly crushed garlic cloves.

Tough

Cakes or muffins can become 'tough' if you mix the dry ingredients into the wet ingredients too much or too vigorously. This makes the cake harder and drier, and not as soft and moist as it should be.

Turn (onto)

To remove a baked product from its pan by loosening the edges (between the baking and sides of the pan) and turning the pan upside down, carefully turning the food onto a wire rack, cutting board or serving plate.

Well

To make a bowl shape in the dry ingredients in a bowl so you can add wet ingredients and gradually mix them together.

Whip

To beat food, like cream to make whipped cream, rapidly to make it light and fluffy using an electric mixer or an egg beater.

Whisk

To beat air into a mixture, using a wire whisk rather than an eggbeater, to increase the volume. This is a gentler method of mixing ingredients than beating.

CARE WITH KNIVES

THE 10 GOLDEN RULES FOR USING AND CARING FOR KNIVES

ALWAYS . . .

1. Carry knives with the point down and blade facing backwards.

2. Pass a knife to another person handle first, not point first.

3. Place knives on benches with the cutting edge facing away and not hanging over the edge.

4. Hold food you are cutting with your fingers tucked in towards your wrist. Watch out for your thumb.

5. Be extra careful when cutting cold foods (0–2°C). Cool temperatures will numb your fingers and you may lose the feeling and easily cut yourself.

6. When cutting a round item (onion, carrot, etc) cut a flat edge and place the item flat edge down to prevent it rolling, and your knife from slipping.

7. Cut your food on a board. You should use different boards for raw and cooked foods. Thoroughly clean boards after use.

8. Wipe a knife with the cutting edge pointing away from your hand.

9. Rinse knives immediately after use, wash in hot soapy water, dry thoroughly and return to storage.

10. Store knives in a block, knife sleeve inside a knife roll or magnetic holder. Never place in a drawer. If using a knife roll use edge guards for extra protection.

Get a grown-up to help you with tricky recipes where you need to use sharp knives or hot things.

BEFORE YOU START . . .

- Read the recipe carefully.

- Make sure you have all the ingredients you need.

- Put the ingredients on your bench within easy reach.

- Get out all the cooking equipment you are going to use e.g. knives, bowls, measuring spoons and cups, baking dishes and trays, frying pan etc.

- Get an adult to check that you have the right knives for the right job.

- If you are going to use the oven, put the oven racks in the right place before you preheat it. Use the top racks for quicker cooking on a higher heat (200°C or higher), the middle ones for moderate heat (about 180°C), and those in the lower oven for slower cooking (150°C or lower).

- If any vegetables or other ingredients need to be prepared beforehand, do this first.

- Wear an apron, especially if it looks as if things will get a bit messy.

NOW . . .

Wash your hands well with soap and water and let's get cooking!

CKC

- Put away all the ingredients you didn't use.

- Put your vegetable peelings on the compost heap, if you have one.

- Put all the other food scraps in the right rubbish bins.

- Wash up all the dishes you have used, dry them and put them back in the right cupboards and drawers.

- Wipe down all the benches and hang up any damp tea towels you have used.

- Check that you have turned off the oven, if you used it, and any elements on the stove.

THEN . . .

Treat yourself to a wee taste of what you've just made.

YUM!

BREAKFASTS AND SNACKS

FRENCH TOAST

INGREDIENTS

4 eggs
4 tablespoons low-fat milk
1 teaspoon sugar
pinch salt for seasoning
pinch cinnamon
4 slices wholemeal bread, toast
    slice thickness
2 teaspoons margarine, for frying

TOPPING CHOICES:

sliced banana and runny honey
maple syrup and grilled bacon,
    with fat and rind removed
low-sugar jam or marmalade
peanut butter

SERVES 4

1. Put the eggs, milk, sugar, salt and cinnamon into a medium-sized bowl and beat together with a fork or eggbeater.

2. Dip 2 slices of bread in the egg mixture so that it soaks into the bread.

3. Melt one teaspoon of the margarine in a frying pan and cook the bread over a medium heat for 2–3 minutes each side until golden brown.

4. Dip the other 2 slices of bread in the egg mixture.

5. Cook in the frying pan as before, using the second teaspoon of margarine to grease the pan if you need it.

6. Slice the French toast in half and serve immediately with the topping of your choice.

HANDY HINT

This is a sweet version but you can make savoury versions by leaving out the sugar in the egg mixture and adding some finely diced onion and a little grated cheese.

Nutty Muesli

Ingredients

2 cups rolled oats
½ cup wheatgerm
½ cup desiccated coconut
½ cup sunflower seeds
½ cup pumpkin seeds
½ cup peanuts or any other
 chopped nuts (i.e. nut mix)
½ cup raisins
¼ cup runny honey
2 tablespoons vegetable oil
½ cup dried apricots, chopped
½ cup dried apple, chopped

Makes 6 cups of Muesli

1. Preheat the oven to 180°C.

2. Combine all the dry ingredients, except the dried fruit, in a large ovenproof dish.

3. Warm the honey and oil together either in a small saucepan over a medium heat on the stove, or in a heatproof bowl in the microwave for 30 seconds. Mix it together with a fork.

4. Drizzle the honey and oil mixture over the dry ingredients and mix thoroughly with your hands until mixture is evenly dampened. Make sure you break up large lumps, as these will go hard when baked.

Handy Hint

This muesli is great with Orange Yoghurt (see opposite) poured on top. The yoghurt is also good served with your favourite cake, instead of whipped cream.

TOPPING

5. Now place the muesli into the oven using your oven mitts and bake for 15 minutes. It is useful here to use an oven timer.

6. Using your oven mitts again, take the muesli out of the oven (you may need help with this) and give it a good stir using a fish slice.

7. Place back in the oven and cook for a further 10 minutes, then repeat the process above — give the muesli another good stir and place it back in the oven for a further 8 minutes, then remove and stir again. If it does not look quite cooked, stir and place back in oven for another 5–10 minutes. The muesli is done when it is a light golden brown.

8. Leave it to cool, then add the chopped dried fruit and stir in well. Store in an airtight container or resealable bag.

ORANGE YOGHURT

1 cup plain unsweetened low-fat yoghurt

¼ cup unsweetened orange juice (fresh is good)

Combine both ingredients in a bowl and mix well.

SERVES 2

OATY PANCAKES

INGREDIENTS

½ cup flour
2 teaspoons baking powder
¾ cup oat bran or rolled oats
½ teaspoon salt
2 teaspoons sugar
2 eggs
¾ cup low-fat milk
2 teaspoons oil
cooking oil spray or a little
  extra oil, for frying

SERVES 4

1. Sift the flour and baking powder into a medium-sized bowl, then add the oats, salt and sugar.

2. In a separate bowl mix eggs, milk, oil and beat well.

3. Make a well in the middle of the dry ingredients. Add the egg mixture and combine well with a wooden spoon. Add a little extra milk if your mixture is too thick.

HANDY HINT

These are American-style pancakes, which have a lovely oaty flavour. Serve them with grilled bacon, runny honey, maple syrup, banana or any other fresh fruit. Your friends will love them!

4. Lightly spray a frying pan with cooking spray, place on an element and set on a high heat.

5. Pour a spoonful of the pancake mixture into the heated frying pan and spread it evenly to make a round pancake.

6. Cook until bubbles appear on top and the underside is golden brown.

7. Flip carefully with a fish slice. Make sure your pan does not get too hot or you will burn the pancakes.

8. Repeat this process until you have cooked all your pancakes. You may have to spray your frying pan again with cooking oil if the pancakes start to stick.

Vanilla Yoghurt

Ingredients

4 cups boiled water
1¼ cups low-fat milk powder
3 teaspoons sugar
pinch of salt
½ cup plain unsweetened low-fat
  yoghurt
1 teaspoon vanilla essence

Serves 4

1. Boil the water and leave to cool until it is lukewarm.

2. Put one cup of this water into a clean jar, then stir in the milk powder with a fork and make sure there are no lumps.

3. Stir in the sugar and salt.

4. Put the plain yoghurt into a cup and mix in a little of the leftover warm water.

5. Stir this mixture into your milk in the jar, add the vanilla essence, then fill the jar with the rest of the warm water.

6. Stir well, then screw on the jar lid.

7. Wrap a few layers of newspaper around the jar and stand in a warm place for 8 hours — a hot water cupboard is perfect. If you don't have a hot water cupboard you can use easily, stand the jar in a bowl of hot water, but you will need to keep replacing the hot water as it cools.

8. When ready, store the yoghurt in the refrigerator.

HANDY HINT

You can flavour your yoghurt with unsweetened fruit pulp. It's also great with muesli or any breakfast cereal, or just with a bowl of fresh fruit.

ANTS ON A LOG

INGREDIENTS

4 stalks of celery
½ cup peanut butter
¼ cup raisins or currants

SERVES 6

1. Wash the celery and cut the stalks into pieces about 10 centimetres long.

2. Using a flat knife, spread peanut butter into the hollow of the celery stalks.

3. Press raisins into the peanut butter.

4. Place filled celery stalks on plate and enjoy!

HANDY HINT

This is a fun, easy and healthy after-school snack.

32

TREKKING MIX

1. Place all the ingredients into a bowl.

2. Mix everything together.

3. Scoop into a small resealable bag, so it's handy when you want a quick snack.

INGREDIENTS

½ cup raisins
½ cup natural or unsalted peanuts
½ cup other mixed nuts (i.e. Brazil nuts, walnuts)
¼ cup dried apricots, chopped
¼ cup dried banana chips
¼ cup shredded or flaked coconut

SERVES 2

Be careful of food allergies — many people are allergic to things like nuts. Make sure that the people you are cooking for don't have any allergies which could make them sick if they ate the wrong thing.

COOL TiP

33

BISKETTI SCRAMBLE

INGREDIENTS

3 eggs
2 tablespoons low-fat milk
pinch each of salt and pepper
1 tablespoon oil
1 medium-sized onion, chopped
1 green capsicum, chopped
½ x 450 g can spaghetti
2 tablespoons grated tasty
  cheese

SERVES 4

1. Beat the eggs, milk, salt and pepper in a small bowl with a fork or whisk and set aside.

2. Heat the oil in a large frying pan (that is also safe to use in the oven) over a medium heat.

3. Cook the chopped onion and green capsicum in the oil, stirring well with a spoon until they are soft and clear, but have not browned.

4. Add the spaghetti to the onion and capsicum and heat until it is warmed through.

5. Pour the egg and milk mixture over the hot spaghetti.

6. Lift the spaghetti with a fish slice so the egg mixture can run underneath. Keep cooking it carefully, but do not stir more than necessary. Be careful not to burn the bottom. Your egg should still be a bit runny on top.

7. Turn on the grill.

8. Take the frying pan off the element and sprinkle the spaghetti with the grated cheese. Using oven mitts, place the scramble under the grill leaving the door open slightly. Grill for a couple of minutes until the cheese has browned.

9. Take out from under the grill and leave to cool for a minute or two before serving it.

JOKE

Q: What are two things you can't have for breakfast?
A: Lunch and dinner!

35

BRUSCHETTA

INGREDIENTS

1 loaf French bread, or 6 slices
   plain bread
1 clove garlic
6 medium-sized tomatoes
¼ teaspoon salt
¼ teaspoon ground pepper
2 tablespoons oil
juice of ½ lemon
2 tablespoons chopped fresh
   basil leaves, or 2 teaspoons
   of dried basil leaves
extra oil, for drizzling

SERVES 6

1. Preheat oven to 180°C

2. Slice the bread diagonally
into 1-centimetre slices and
then toast in the oven for
approximately 10 minutes
until they are lightly toasted.
Be careful not to burn them!

3. Peel and crush a clove of garlic.

4. Dice 4–6 medium-sized
tomatoes using a serrated
knife, or you can slice them if
it's easier, and place them into a
bowl with the crushed garlic.

5. Mix in salt and pepper,
1 tablespoon of the oil and
the lemon juice.

6. Add chopped fresh basil leaves or
dried basil.

7. Spread the tomato mixture on the
toasted bread and drizzle with a few
tablespoons of the extra oil.

HANDY HINT

A crusty white bread, like French bread, works best for making Bruschetta.

EZY BREAD

INGREDIENTS

2 cups wholemeal flour

2 cups white flour

1 tablespoon salt

1 tablespoon runny honey

1 tablespoon dried yeast

2½ cups warm water

½ can corn kernels, drained (optional)

2 tablespoons chopped parsley (optional)

¼ cup grated tasty cheese (optional)

SERVES 8

1. Preheat your oven to 200°C.

2. Sift wholemeal flour, white flour and salt into a large mixing bowl.

3. Make a well in the middle of the flour and pour in the honey and yeast.

4. Then pour in warm water and stir until combined. The dough will be quite sticky.

5. Cover with a clean damp tea towel and place somewhere warm, like a hot water cupboard, to 'prove' for 45 minutes, or until doubled in size.

6. Once your dough has doubled in size, stir it a few times so that it sinks down. Add any optional ingredients at this stage.

7. Turn into a greased, medium-sized loaf tin — it should be about three-quarters full — and bake at 200°C for 40–45 minutes.

8. Turn out onto a wire rack to cool.

An easy way to pour flour and other dry ingredients is to sift them on to a sheet of lunch paper. You can then just fold the paper over to make a funnel and tip the flour into the wet ingredients a little at a time.

Cool Tip

39

MOUSETRAPS

INGREDIENTS

8 slices wholemeal bread
2 tablespoons Marmite
1½ cups grated tasty cheese

SERVES 4

1. Lightly toast wholemeal bread in the toaster.

2. Slice the crusts off the bread, if you like, and lay it on an oven tray.

3. Turn on the grill.

4. Spread the Marmite evenly over the toast and sprinkle with cheese.

5. Using oven mitts, place the tray under the grill.

6. Grill on high for 5–8 minutes until cheese has bubbled and turned crispy.

7. Remove from the grill and slice each piece of toast into 3 strips.

8. Eat warm, or if you can resist the temptation, allow to cool and store in an airtight container.

POPCORN

INGREDIENTS

1 tablespoon margarine
½ cup popping corn
salt to season

SWEET TOPPING:

¼ cup brown sugar
2 tablespoons raisins or dried
    apricots
1 teaspoon cinnamon

SERVES 4

1. Melt margarine in a medium to large saucepan on a medium heat, until sizzling.

2. Put popcorn into saucepan, cover with a tight-fitting lid and cook on a high heat until popcorn starts to pop!

3. Once this starts to happen, turn the heat down to medium-low and wait until the corn stops popping. Make sure you lift your saucepan from the heat occasionally and give it a good shake to prevent burning. It's best to use oven mitts to do this as the saucepan will be hot.

4. Place your popcorn into a bowl and season with salt.

COOL TIP

You can use a popcorn machine to pop your popcorn instead of a saucepan. Just follow the manufacturer's instructions.

HANDY HINT

If you want to make your popcorn into a sweetened version, sprinkle with the sweet topping ingredients.

TRIPLE-DECKER SANDWICHES

INGREDIENTS

3 eggs
salt and pepper
4 slices white bread
8 slices brown bread
approx 2 tablespoons low-fat
    mayonnaise (enough to spread
    thinly on 4 slices of bread)
approx 100 g thinly shaved ham
    (enough to cover 4 slices of
    bread)
2 teaspoons margarine
3 tomatoes, thinly sliced
½ small lettuce, shredded
½ cup grated tasty cheese

SERVES 4

1. Hard boil the eggs by cooking them in a saucepan of boiling water for 10 minutes. Cool them under cold water, then peel and mash them up in a small bowl with a fork. Season with salt and pepper.

2. Lay 4 slices of brown bread on a chopping board and spread them thinly with mayonnaise and top each with a slice of ham.

3. Divide the egg mixture and spread over the 4 slices of bread.

4. Top each sandwich base with a piece of white bread and spread thinly with margarine.

5. Lay slices of tomato on the 4 pieces of bread, then a layer of shredded lettuce and another of cheese.

6. Top each sandwich with your final pieces of brown bread then cut the sandwiches in half or diagonally.

45

VEGGIE SUNDAE

INGREDIENTS

FOR THE DRESSING:

3 teaspoons cider vinegar
1 teaspoon runny honey
3 teaspoons oil
¼ cup chopped fresh basil or
    1 teaspoon dried basil
salt and pepper

FOR THE SUNDAE:

2 stalks celery, chopped
2 carrots, grated
1 cucumber, diced
1 cup cherry tomatoes, sliced
    in half (or use chopped
    normal tomatoes)

SERVES 4

To make the dressing:

1. Place the cider and runny honey into a mixing bowl and mix with a fork or a whisk.

2. Slowly drizzle in the oil, mixing all the time with a fork or whisk.

3. Add chopped fresh basil. You can use dried basil, but don't use quite as much as dried herbs have a stronger flavour than fresh herbs.

4. Add a dash of salt and pepper.

To make the sundae:

1. Peel and wash the vegetables

2. Chop them into small pieces. Be sure to check with a grown-up before you do this.

3. Put a layer of each vegetable into a glass cup or beaker, so you can see all the colours. Use 4 small glasses or 2 large ones.

4. Pour some of your homemade dressing over the vegetables to add some punch to the crunch.

HANDY HINT

This is a fun way to eat your veggies! You can also use other colourful veggies, such as green, red or yellow capsicums, or even finely shredded red cabbage.

47

Chicken + Sweetcorn Soup

Ingredients

1 boneless chicken breast, skin removed

3 cups liquid chicken stock, or make up your own using dried chicken stock

2 tablespoons cornflour (plus approx ¼ cup cold water to mix)

300 g can cream-style sweetcorn

salt and freshly ground black pepper

SERVES 3-4

I. Cut chicken into tiny pieces. Set aside. Be sure to check with an adult before you do this.

2. Bring chicken stock to the boil in a medium-sized saucepan, stirring constantly until it comes to boil.

3. Add chicken and corn. Simmer for 3–4 minutes until chicken is cooked and soup is hot, stirring all the time.

4. In a cup, combine the cornflour with just enough water to make a smooth paste, stirring until it goes nice and smooth.

5. Add this paste to the hot soup and stir for a further minute until it thickens. If it is not thick enough just mix another 2 teaspoons of cornflour with a little more water to form a paste. Add to hot soup and cook for a little longer.

6. Season to taste with salt and pepper.

7. Ladle into warm bowls and serve with Ezy Bread (see recipe on page 38).

HANDY HINT

This soup is really yummy and is a great way to warm yourself up on a cold winter's day.

49

MAIN MEALS

BACON + VEGGIE SLAB

3 rashers bacon, trimmed of rind and fat and finely chopped

2 carrots, peeled and grated

2 zucchini, grated

½ x 400 g can drained corn kernels

1 medium-sized onion, diced

½ cup tasty grated cheese

4 eggs

¼ cup oil

1 teaspoon baking powder

⅓ cup flour

1 teaspoon dried basil or marjoram

½ teaspoon salt plus a shake of pepper

1 teaspoon margarine for greasing, or non-stick cooking spray

SERVES 4-6

1. Preheat the oven to 180°C.

2. Trim and chop the bacon and prepare all the vegetables. Grate the cheese.

3. Put the eggs, oil and baking powder into a medium-sized bowl and mix well with a fork or whisk.

4. Sift the flour and add together with all the other ingredients.

5. Stir to combine well.

6. Pour your mixture into a greased shallow pie dish or any other medium-sized baking dish. You can also use a quiche dish if you like. Pat it flat with a spatula.

7. Bake for 30–35 minutes until golden brown and set. The slice will be firm to touch when it is cooked.

Get a grown-up to help you with tricky recipes where you need to use sharp knives and hot things.

COOL TiP

HAMBURGERS

INGREDIENTS

FOR THE BURGER PATTIES:

1 teaspoon oil

1 medium-sized onion, diced

½ cup wholemeal breadcrumbs, or
substitute ½ cup rolled oats

500 g lean mince, e.g. beef, lamb
or pork

1 egg

2–4 tablespoons tomato sauce (or
any savoury sauce or relish)

salt and pepper

1 tablespoon extra oil for
frying patties

1. Preheat oven to 180°C.

2. Heat 1 teaspoon of oil in a
frying pan and fry the onion
for a few minutes until soft.
Leave to cool.

3. In a glass bowl, mix the
breadcrumbs with the mince
meat, egg and tomato sauce
until well combined. Season
with salt and pepper. Then add
the cooled onions.

4. Shape the mincemeat mixture
into 6 patties and place on a plate.

5. Heat the extra tablespoon of oil in a large frying pan over a medium to high heat and fry your burger patties on each side until browned.

6. Then place the patties onto an oven tray and bake for 10–15 minutes, until cooked through. Your burgers are cooked when the meat is no longer pink in the middle.

7. Split the burger buns in half and grill them in the oven, cut side up, until lightly toasted. Be careful you don't burn them!

8. Squirt one side of your bun with low-fat mayonnaise and the other side with tomato sauce, or with whatever spread you like most.

9. Fill your bun with a burger pattie, some sliced tomato, beetroot, cheese and lettuce.

FOR THE BURGERS:

6 wholemeal or wholegrain hamburger buns
tasty cheese, sliced
2 tomatoes, thinly sliced
1 lettuce, broken into leaves and washed
½ can sliced beetroot, drained (optional)

FOR SPREADING ON THE BUNS:

tomato sauce or relish
low-fat mayonnaise
American-style mustard, in a squeeze bottle

SERVES 6

55

CKC Pizza

INGREDIENTS

PIZZA DOUGH:

1 tablespoon active yeast
½ teaspoon sugar
1 cup warm water
1 teaspoon salt
¾ cup high grade white flour
¾ cup wholemeal flour
1 tablespoon oil

MAKES 2 MEDIUM-SIZED PIZZAS ENOUGH FOR 8-10 PEOPLE

To make the dough from scratch:

1. Preheat oven to 220°C.

2. Combine yeast, sugar and water in a bowl. Set aside in a warm place for 15 minutes until frothy.

3. Combine salt and flour in a large bowl.

4. Add yeast mixture and oil and mix until ingredients form a soft dough.

5. Transfer the dough to a lightly floured surface. Knead for 5 minutes until smooth and elastic.

6. Lightly oil a large bowl. Sit dough in the bowl and cover with a clean tea towel. Stand in a warm place to 'prove' until the dough doubles in size, about 45 minutes.

7. Lightly grease an oven tray with cooking oil. If you do not have a tray large enough for two bases you will need to use two trays.

TOPPINGS

8. Push your fist into the middle of the dough to knock it down. Transfer to a lightly floured surface. Knead for 1 minute.

9. Cut the dough into 2 equal pieces. Roll each piece into a 30-centimetre diameter circle to form the pizza bases.

10. Place the bases on the greased oven tray or trays and spread them with tomato paste.

11. Top with a selection of your favourite combination of toppings from the list on the right — most people like to finish with a good sprinkling of cheese.

12. Bake for 10 minutes in preheated oven, or until golden brown.

PIZZA TOPPING OPTIONS:

4 teaspoons tomato paste
1 medium-sized onion, diced
1 cup diced ham
1 cup drained canned unsweetened crushed pineapple
1 cup cooked chicken, shredded
½ x 400 g can whole kernel corn, drained
1 cup mushrooms, sliced
1 x 400g can tuna in brine or spring water, drained
3 medium tomatoes, sliced thinly
1 cup grated tasty cheese or Mozzarella cheese

HANDY HINT

You can buy pizza bases. Use 4 x 30-centimetre diameter pizza bases to make four pizzas. Pita bread is also fantastic to use as bases.

57

FiSH FiNGERS

iNGREDiENTS

4 fillets fleshy white fish (fresh or
    frozen, we used terakihi)
½ cup flour
1 cup dried breadcrumbs
salt and pepper
1 egg
1 tablespoon low-fat milk
1½ tablespoons oil
4 lemon wedges, to serve
tomato sauce, to serve

SERVES 4

1. Cut your fish fillets into finger-length strips.

2. Spread the flour and breadcrumbs out on two separate plates, and season the flour with salt and pepper.

3. Break the egg into a bowl, add the milk and mix together using a fork or whisk.

4. Coat the fish fingers with flour, then dip them into the egg mixture. Then coat them well on both sides with the breadcrumbs.

5. Heat the oil in a frying pan over a medium heat and add the fish fingers. Fry for 3–4 minutes on each side until browned on the outside but cooked in the middle. The fish fingers are cooked when the fish flakes easily when tested with a fork and the flesh has turned white.

6. If the outsides of the fish fingers are brown but the insides are not quite cooked, you can finish them off by placing them on a tray and baking them for 5 minutes at 180°C in a preheated oven.

HANDY HINT

Serve your fish fingers with tomato sauce or a good squeeze of juice from a wecge of lemon.

IRISH STEW

INGREDIENTS

1 kg mutton or lamb shoulder
   chops or 750 g leg chops
salt and pepper
4 large potatoes, peeled and sliced
2 large onions, sliced
2 stalks celery, sliced
1 cup frozen mixed vegetables
1–2 teaspoons instant chicken
   stock
1 tablespoon Worcestershire
   sauce
2 tablespoons chopped parsley
1 tablespoon cornflour mixed
   with a little water to make
   a paste

SERVES 4-6

I. Remove all the fat and gristle from the chops — you will need help from an adult to do this. Place the lamb in a medium to large saucepan and cover with water. Season with salt and pepper and simmer on a low heat for an hour with the lid on.

2. Let the stew cool, then skim off any excess fat.

3. Peel and slice the potatoes thickly and place on top of the chops.

4. Over the potatoes, place layers of sliced onion and celery, followed by the frozen vegetables.

5. Cover with a lid and simmer on a medium to low heat for 1 hour, until the meat is tender and the veggies are cooked, but not mushy.

HANDY HINT

Try serving your stew with mint sauce.

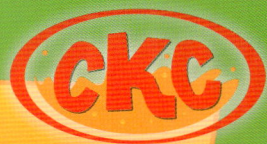

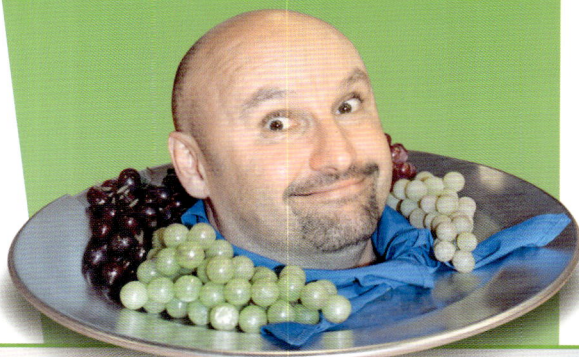

6. Taste your stew and season with instant chicken stock and Worcestershire sauce if it does not have enough flavour.

7. Add half the chopped parsley and the cornflour mixture, stir and simmer for a couple of minutes until thickened

8. Top with the rest of the parsley and serve in individual bowls.

JOKE

Q: What do you get if you cross a Roman emperor with an orange?

A: Julius Squeezer!

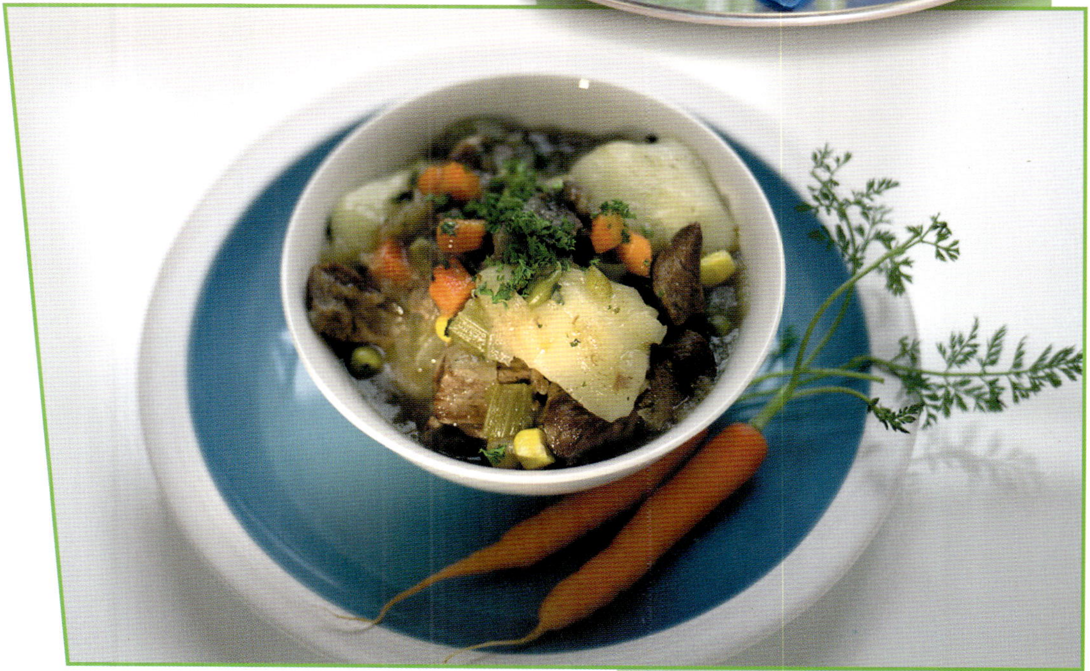

¡SLAND CHOP SUEY

iNGREDiENTS

1 x 125 g packet rice vermicelli
1 cup hot water, to soak vermicelli
1 tablespoon oil
250 g diced lean beef, pork or
  chicken
2 cloves garlic, crushed using a
  garlic crusher, or use crushed
  garlic from a jar
1 tablespoon finely chopped
  fresh ginger, or crushed
  ginger from a jar
1 medium-sized onion,
  finely chopped
200 g carrots, diced
200 g button mushrooms,
  sliced
½ cup water
6 tablespoons soy sauce

SERVES 4-6

1. Place the vermicelli in a medium-sized bowl, cover with hot water and leave to soak until soft.

2. Drain the vermicelli and when cool, chop it into approximately 20-centimetre length pieces.

3. Heat the oil in a large saucepan or wok, on a medium to high heat. Add the meat, garlic, ginger and onion and stir-fry until the meat is nicely browned. Be careful not to burn your meat.

4. Then add the carrots and mushrooms and stir-fry for a further 4–5 minutes.

5. Add the vermicelli, the ½ cup of water and soy sauce to your stir-fry. Cover with a lid and simmer for 15 minutes, over a low heat, stirring every few minutes, until the meat is tender. You may have to add a bit more water to prevent the chop suey from sticking.

6. Serve with a green salad or vegetables.

KUMARA OR POTATO BOATS

INGREDIENTS

4 medium to large kumara or
    potatoes, washed but not peeled
salt and pepper
grated tasty cheese, for garnish

FILLING OPTION 1:

210 g can smoked fish or tuna in
    spring water or savoury sauce
125 g cottage cheese
½ can sweetcorn kernels,
    drained
1 spring onion, chopped

FILLING OPTION 2:

5 thin slices ham, chopped
125 g crushed pineapple,
    drained
¼ cup grated tasty cheese

SERVES 4

1. Preheat oven to 200°C.

2. Bake your kumara or
    potatoes in the oven, on an
    oven tray, for 30 minutes or
    until soft. Potatoes will take
    longer than kumara to cook.

3. Remove them from the oven
    and leave to cool for a while.

4. Slice off the top of each kumara
    or potato. Keep the tops to one
    side to use later.

5. Scoop out the cooked middle using
    a dessertspoon and place into a
    bowl. Try not to break the skin.

6. Mash the kumara or potato a
    little with a wooden spoon, then
    stir in whichever filling you like
    most. Season the mixture with salt
    and pepper.

7. Stuff the filling into the kumara or
    potato skins and sprinkle with a little
    extra cheese.

8. Put the tops back on the 'boats' and
    bake in the oven for 10–15 minutes,
    until the cheese is melted and they are
    well heated through.

HANDY HINT

You can divide the kumara or potato between two bowls if you want to use two cifferent fillings.

MARVELLOUS MEATBALLS

INGREDIENTS

1 teaspoon oil

1 medium-sized onion, finely chopped

1 capsicum, seeded and finely chopped

2 carrots, washed, peeled and grated

500 g low-fat beef or pork mince

1 egg

1. Preheat oven to 200°C.

2. Heat 1 teaspoon of oil in a frying pan and lightly fry the onions and capsicum for 5 minutes until tender.

3. Place grated carrot, the mince and all the other ingredients, except the pasta sauce, into a medium-sized bowl and mix well. You might need to use your hands to do this.

4. Lightly spray an oven tray with cooking oil spray or grease lightly with cooking oil, applying with a paper towel.

5. Roll the meat mixture into balls about 3 centimetres round in size, and place them on the oven tray as you go.

COOL TIP

There are various types of parsley available. You can either use curly parsley or the flat-leaved type, which is sometimes known as Italian parsley.

MORE INGREDIENTS

6. Bake for 8–10 minutes or until cooked through. You can check this by cutting one open and making sure it is not pink in the middle.

7. Heat the pasta sauce in a saucepan or in the microwave until well heated through.

8. Pour the warmed pasta sauce over your meatballs. They are great served with spaghetti and a green salad (see recipe on page 85).

½ teaspoon salt
1 teaspoon ground black pepper
½ cup soft or dried wholemeal breadcrumbs
4 sprigs parsley, chopped
1 x 400 g jar tomato pasta sauce

SERVES 4

Nachos

INGREDIENTS

1 tablespoon oil
1 medium-sized onion, chopped
500 g lean beef mince or shredded
    chicken
2 cloves garlic, crushed
1 teaspoon ground cumin
½ teaspoon ground coriander
400 g can whole peeled
    tomatoes, in juice
2 tablespoons tomato paste
1 teaspoon garlic or green herb
    stock
½ cup water
salt and pepper
4–6 drops Tabasco sauce
1 x 420 g can kidney beans,
    drained
1 x 200 g bag corn chips
½ cup cheddar cheese,
    grated
100 g light sour cream

SERVES 6

1. Heat the oil in a frying pan
   and cook the onion for
   5 minutes until soft.

2. Add the mince, garlic and
   spices and cook until mince is
   browned, stirring for about
   10 minutes.

3. Add tomatoes, tomato paste,
   stock and water, breaking up
   tomatoes with a wooden spoon.
   Cook over a low heat for 25–30
   minutes until sauce is thick.

4. Season to taste with salt, pepper
   and 4–5 drops of Tabasco sauce.
   (This is a very hot and spicy sauce,
   so be careful not to add too much,
   and do not get it near your eyes.)
   Taste and add another drop of
   Tabasco if you think it needs it.

5. Add beans and stir gently for
   1–2 minutes, or until well heated
   through.

6. Scatter the corn chips over the base of
   an ovenproof dish.

7. Turn the oven grill on.

8. Spoon the mince mixture over the chips.

9. Sprinkle with cheese. Grill for 3–4 minutes until cheese melts and bubbles.

10. Serve with sour cream and a fresh green salad.

69

PACIFIC PATTIES

INGREDIENTS

1½ cups taro, peeled
2 rashers lean bacon
1 teaspoon baking powder, sifted
1 x 340 g can of low-fat corned
   beef
1 egg
½ cup wholemeal flour
pinch salt and pepper
1 cup dried breadcrumbs
2 tablespoons oil

SERVES 6

1. Chop the taro into medium-sized pieces and boil in a saucepan until soft and tender, about 35–40 minutes (it takes a lot longer to cook than potato). When the taro is cooked, put to one side to cool.

2. Trim the bacon by cutting off the rind and fat.

3. Place your bacon on an absorbent paper towel and cook in the microwave on high for 1–2 minutes. Alternatively, preheat oven to 180°C, put the bacon on a baking tray, place in the oven using oven mitts, and cook for 5 minutes. Make sure you watch your bacon so it doesn't burn!

4. Let your bacon cool, and then chop finely.

5. Once the taro is cool, mash it with a potato masher. Transfer it to a bowl and combine with the sifted baking powder, cooked bacon, corned beef and egg. Mix well using a spoon.

6. Add the flour to the taro pattie mixture, season with salt and pepper and mix well.

7. Roll the mixture into small balls about the size of a ping-pong ball and squash flat, making them about 5 centimetres round. Repeat the process until you have used up all of your mixture.

8. Place the breadcrumbs on a plate. Dip your patties into the breadcrumbs, make sure they are completely coated on both sides.

9. Heat a small amount of oil in a frying pan, over a medium heat. You'll know the oil is hot enough if it sizzles when you place your pattie into the frying pan. Using kitchen tongs add the patties, three or four at a time, and cook on each side until golden brown.

10. Remove patties from the frying pan and drain on absorbent paper towels.

11. Serve with a green salad and warm salsa or tomato sauce on the side.

Pizza Kebabs

Ingredients

8 skewers
½ loaf French bread, cubed
100 g sliced salami
1 green capsicum, cut into bite-sized pieces
8 fresh mushrooms, halved
1 zucchini, cut into 1–2 centimetre slices
¼ cup low-fat Italian dressing
¼ cup grated tasty cheese
½ cup mild tomato salsa, warmed, or tomato sauce, for dipping

Makes 8 kebabs

1. If you are using bamboo skewers, soak them in water for at least half an hour before using them. This will stop them from burning when you are cooking the kebabs.

2. Preheat oven to 180°C.

3. Put the cubed bread onto an oven tray and lightly toast in the oven for about 5–10 minutes, making sure you don't burn it.

4. Thread the salami, bread, and prepared veggies onto the skewers, in various combinations.

5. Place a sheet of baking paper on baking tray. Arrange skewers in a single layer on the tray.

6. Brush lightly with the Italian dressing and sprinkle each with a little cheese.

7. Bake for 20 minutes, until heated through and cheese has melted.

HANDY HINT

Serve with a green salad (see page 85) and use warm salsa or tomato sauce for dipping.

Sesame Chicken Bits

Ingredients

2 boneless chicken breasts, skin removed
2 tablespoons soy sauce
2 tablespoons runny honey
3 teaspoons oil
1 teaspoon sesame oil (optional)
¾ cup sesame seeds

SERVES 4

1. Preheat oven to 220°C.

2. Cut chicken into 1.5-centimetre wide strips. Put into a medium-sized bowl.

3. Place soy sauce, honey and oil into a bowl and mix well.

4. Pour it over the chicken and mix through until the chicken is evenly coated.

5. Cover with plastic wrap and refrigerate for 30 minutes. This lets the chicken marinate and soak up the yummy soy and honey flavours.

6. Put the sesame seeds onto a flat plate.

7. Take the chicken strips out of the marinade and roll them in the sesame seeds until they are well coated.

8. Place the strips in a lightly oiled roasting dish.

9. Bake at 220°C for 15 minutes, turning every 4–5 minutes, until chicken is cooked.

How do you tell if chicken is cooked properly? Cut open a baked chicken bit and if it has no pink flesh and has turned white, then it is cooked.

COOL TiP

SPAGHETTI BOLOGNESE

INGREDIENTS

1 tablespoon oil
1 medium-sized onion, chopped
500 g lean minced beef
2 cloves garlic, crushed
1 teaspoon dried basil
½ teaspoon dried oregano
400 g can whole peeled or diced
   tomatoes
2 tablespoons tomato paste
½ teaspoon sugar
salt and pepper
300 g dried spaghetti
grated parmesan or tasty
   cheese, to serve

SERVES 4

1. Heat oil in a frying pan and cook the onion for about 5 minutes until soft.

2. Add mince, garlic and herbs to the onions and continue to cook until the mince is browned, stirring for about 10 minutes.

3. Add the tomatoes, tomato paste and sugar, breaking up tomatoes with a wooden spoon.

4. Turn the heat down to low and cook for a further 30–35 minutes, until the sauce is thick.

5. Season to taste with salt and pepper.

6. About 15 minutes before sauce is cooked, half fill a large saucepan with water.

HANDY HINT

Offer grated parmesan or tasty cheese to sprinkle over the meat sauce. Serve with a fresh green salad (see page 85).

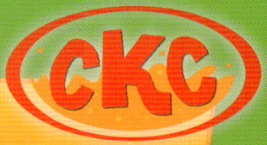

7. Bring water to the boil. Add the spaghetti and stir with a wooden spoon.

8. Boil the spaghetti for 10–12 minutes or until al dente, which means soft but firm to bite into. Drain spaghetti in a sieve.

9. Divide the spaghetti between 4 serving plates and spoon the meat sauce over the top.

joKE

Q: Why did the boy stare hard out at a bottle of fruit juice?

A: 'Cos it said 'concentrate'!

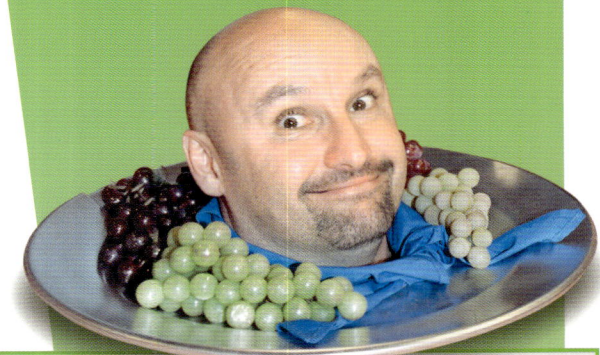

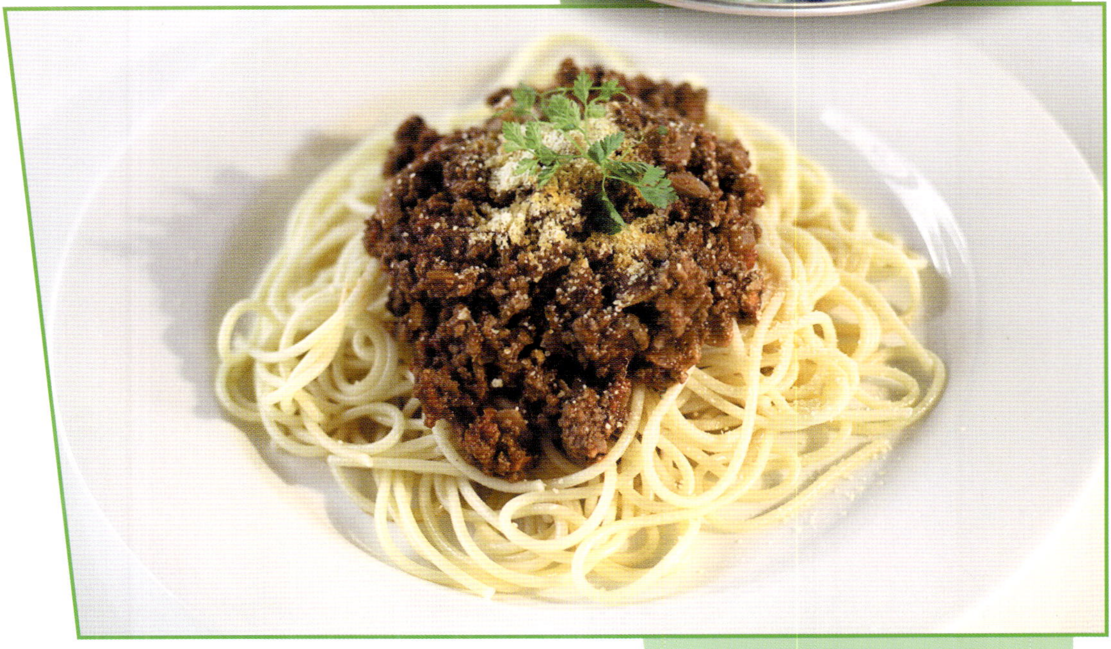

TACOS

INGREDIENTS

MEAT SAUCE:

½ tablespoon oil
½ medium-sized onion, chopped
250 g lean beef or chicken mince
1 clove garlic, crushed
½ teaspoon ground cumin
¼ teaspoon ground coriander
½ teaspoon garlic or green
   herb stock
½ x 400 g can whole peeled
   tomatoes in their juice
1 tablespoon tomato paste
¼ cup water
½ x 400 g can kidney beans
3 drops Tabasco sauce
salt and pepper

1. Preheat oven to 180°C.

2. Heat oil in a frying pan. Cook onion for 5 minutes until soft.

3. Add the mince, garlic, cumin, coriander and stock. Cook until the mince is browned, stirring for about 10 minutes.

4. Add canned tomatoes, tomato paste and water, breaking up tomatoes with a wooden spoon.

5. Cook over a low heat for 25–30 minutes, until sauce is thick.

6. Add the kidney beans to the meat sauce and stir gently for 1–2 minutes to heat them through.

7. Add 3 drops of Tabasco sauce (this is a very hot and spicy sauce, so be careful not to add too much and do not get any near your eyes). Season to taste with salt and pepper.

8. Now place 8 taco shells in the oven for 5 minutes, to warm up. Chop and slice the fresh vegetables and put them in separate bowls to serve.

9. To eat the tacos — fill your taco shell with meat sauce and top it with your favourite ingredients.

MORE INGREDIENTS

FOR SERVING:

8 taco shells
1 lettuce, washed and shredded
2 tomatoes, sliced
1 avocado, peeled and sliced
1 carrot, peeled and grated
½ cup grated tasty cheese
150 g light sour cream

SERVES 8

TUNA CANOES

INGREDIENTS

225 g can tuna in spring water,
   drained
3 tablespoons low-fat mayonnaise
1 spring onion, finely chopped
   (optional)
salt and pepper
4 celery stalks
8 slices green or red capsicum

1. Mix the tuna and mayonnaise together in a bowl. Add the chopped spring onion, season with salt and pepper and mix well again.

2. Wash the celery stalks and trim the ends.

3. To make your canoes, slice a small piece lengthwise off the bottom of each celery stalk. This will keep it from tipping over when it is placed on a plate.

4. Using a spoon, press your tuna salad into the hollow of the celery stalk.

5. Add green or red capsicum sticks to make canoe paddles.

COOL TIP

Lots of recipes ask for a tablespoon or two of an ingredient. If you don't have a standard set of measuring spoons with a tablespoon measure, you can use one of the large tablespoons you usually use for serving food.

ASIAN BROWN RICE SALAD

INGREDIENTS

¾ cup long grain brown rice
approx 1½ cups water
4 spring onions, finely sliced
½ red and green pepper,
    deseeded and sliced
½ cup canned drained corn
    kernels
2 carrots, peeled and grated.

DRESSING:

¼ teaspoon seeded mustard
¼ teaspoon sugar
1 tablespoon wine vinegar or
    cider vinegar
1 tablespoon soy sauce
1 teaspoon sesame oil
salt and pepper

SERVES 4

1. Place rice in a medium-sized saucepan, cover with water and a lid and bring to the boil. Reduce the heat and simmer until water has evaporated and rice is tender (you may have to add a bit more water if it evaporates before the rice is cooked).

2. Place cooked rice in a medium-sized bowl and chill in the refrigerator.

3. While the rice is cooling, prepare all the vegetables.

4. Remove the cooled rice from the refrigerator and add all the vegetables, mixing everything together well.

5. Mix all the dressing ingredients together in a bowl with a whisk and toss through the salad.

COLESLAW

INGREDIENTS

¼ small green cabbage, shredded

¼ red cabbage, shredded (optional)

2 sticks celery, chopped

3 carrots, peeled and grated

¼ cup grated tasty cheese

½ cup chopped chives (optional)

½–¾ cup low-fat mayonnaise.

salt and pepper

2 tablespoons sesame seeds (optional)

2 tablespoons sunflower seeds (optional)

SERVES 4-6

1. Combine the cabbage, celery, carrots, cheese and chives together in a medium-sized bowl.

2. Stir the low-fat mayonnaise thoroughly through the mixture. Season with salt and pepper.

3. Sprinkle with seeds if desired.

1. Combine all your salad ingredients in a large salad bowl.

2. To make salad dressing, combine all ingredients in a small bowl and whisk together, or use a small jar with a lid and shake well.

3. Pour the salad dressing over your salad and toss together carefully.

INGREDIENTS

approx 200 g mesculin (mixed lettuce you buy from the supermarket)
or 1 iceberg lettuce, washed and cut into bite-sized pieces
2 tomatoes, cut into wedges
½ telegraph cucumber, sliced into thin rounds
1 large carrot, peeled and grated (optional)
1 tablespoon sunflower seeds
1 tablespoon pumpkin seeds

DRESSING:

2 tablespoons red wine vinegar or balsamic vinegar (or you can use lemon juice)
½ teaspoon Dijon mustard (optional)
¼ cup oil
1 teaspoon runny honey
pinch salt and pepper

SERVES 4-6

85

KUMARA SALAD

INGREDIENTS

3 large kumara, peeled and cut into
   1-centimetre cubes
2 sticks celery, sliced
1 red onion, peeled, halved and
   sliced
1 avocado, diced (optional)

DRESSING:

¼ cup orange juice
¼ cup low-fat coconut cream
1 teaspoon wine vinegar or
   cider vinegar
1 teaspoon wholegrain
   mustard
pinch of salt

SERVES 6

1. Put the kumara cubes into a saucepan, cover with water and bring to the boil. Cook lightly until the kumara is tender.

2. While the kumara is cooking prepare the vegetables and make the dressing. Mix all the dressing ingredients together in a bowl with a whisk.

3. When the kumara is tender, drain and put into a bowl to cool slightly. While it is still warm, drizzle with the dressing.

4. Add the other vegetables and mix with the kumara, but try not to break up the vegetables too much. Chill the salad in the refrigerator.

5. Serve on a bed of mixed salad leaves.

HANDY HINT

Be careful that you don't overcook the kumara for your salad, otherwise it will break up and be too mushy!

PACIFIC SALAD

INGREDIENTS

2 carrots, peeled and grated
1 cup unsweetened, crushed
   drained pineapple
½ cup shredded coconut
½ cup raisins

SERVES 4

Combine all ingredients in a bowl and chill in the refrigerator for half an hour.

HANDY HINT

This is a light tropical salad which can also be served with plain yoghurt and crackers, or as a side serve with one of your main meals.

PASTA SALAD

1. Cook pasta according to instructions on the packet.

2. Transfer to a sieve. Cool under cold running water, then leave to drain thoroughly.

3. Combine all salad ingredients in a large bowl.

4. To make the dressing, place all ingredients in a small bowl and mix together with a wooden spoon.

5. Spoon the dressing over the pasta mixture and mix gently.

INGREDIENTS

FOR THE SALAD:

150 g dried pasta, e.g. spirals
3 tomatoes, cubed
½ capsicum, diced (optional)
4 gherkins, diced (optional)
100 g tasty cheese, cut into small cubes
½ cup chopped walnuts

DRESSING:

3 tablespoons low-fat mayonnaise
¼ teaspoon Dijon mustard (optional)
1 tablespoon chopped parsley
salt and pepper

SERVES 6

Tuna Salad

Ingredients

For the salad:

3 eggs
250 g fresh green beans
1 yellow or orange capsicum
4 spring onions
1 small lettuce or half a large one
2 tomatoes
½ telegraph cucumber
200 g can tuna in brine, drained

1. Put eggs in a small saucepan and cover with cold water. Bring to the boil and cook for 10 minutes.

2. Take off the heat and run the eggs under cold water.

3. While the eggs are cooling, quarter fill a medium-sized saucepan with water and bring to the boil.

DRESSING

4. Cut the ends off the beans and add to the pan. Boil for 2 minutes. Drain and leave to cool.

5. When the eggs are cool take the shells off and cut into thick slices or quarters.

6. Cut the capsicum into slices and take out the seeds. Chop the spring onions.

7. Wash and dry the lettuce leaves and tear them into bite-sized pieces. Wash the tomatoes and cut them into quarters. Wash and slice the cucumber.

8. Put all the vegetables into a mixing bowl.

9. Add the tuna. Use a fork to flake the fish into the mixing bowl with the salad ingredients. Now add the eggs.

10. Mix the salad dressing ingredients together with a whisk. Pour the dressing over the salad and gently toss to mix the dressing through.

LOW-FAT SALAD DRESSING:

4 tablespoons oil

2 tablespoons cider vinegar

1½ teaspoons sugar

1 teaspoon wholegrain mustard

salt and pepper

SERVES 4

HANDY HINT

Alternatively you could dress your salad with a light French dressing. Salads are great in summer and this one is big enough to feed the whole family.

91

SWEET THINGS

APPLE CRUMBLE

INGREDIENTS

5 apples
4 tablespoons water
pinch of cinnamon
200 g raspberries (you can use the
  frozen variety defrosted) plus
  4 tablespoons sugar or 200 g
  feijoa pulp plus 2 tablespoons
  sugar
¾ cup rolled oats
3 tablespoons wholemeal flour
3 tablespoons desiccated or
  shredded coconut
3 tablespoons chopped
  almonds (optional)
1 tablespoon margarine
3 tablespoons runny honey

SERVES 4

1. Preheat oven to 200°C.

2. Peel, quarter and core the apples.

3. Place the apples in a medium-sized saucepan. Add the water and bring to the boil. Simmer until the apples are soft.

4. Strain off any excess water, then add the cinnamon and either raspberries or feijoas, and the sugar.

5. To make the topping, mix the dry ingredients together in a bowl, then add the margarine and the runny honey.

6. Mix well with your hands until the mixture resembles breadcrumbs.

7. Spoon apple mixture into a medium-sized oven dish and flatten with a spatula.

8. Spread the crumble over fruit and pat down again with the spatula.

9. Cook for 15–20 minutes at 200°C or until top is golden.

HANDY HINT

Apple crumble is delish served with custard. It's a great winter dessert to warm you up.

BANANA ICE CREAM

INGREDIENTS

4 bananas
1 teaspoon runny honey
juice of half an orange
¼ cup toasted coconut (optional)

SERVES 4

1. Peel the bananas and slice them into 2-centimetre slices.

2. Put them in a plastic bag (supermarket bags are good for this) and freeze overnight.

3. Remove bananas from the freezer.

4. Place them in a food processor, with the honey and orange juice and whiz until blended.

5. Scrape the mixture out into a plastic container and refreeze for an hour.

6. Scoop out into bowls, sprinkle with toasted coconut (see Handy Hint opposite) and serve with fresh fruit salad, or in an ice cream cone or as an ice cream sandwich with wafers.

HANDY HINT

To toast the coconut, preheat the oven to 200°C. Put the coconut in an ovenproof dish and toast it for 5–10 minutes, until golden brown, stirring from time to time.

BANANAS ON A STICK

INGREDIENTS

2 x 50 g bars Energy chocolate or
    250 g tub low-fat fruit-flavoured
    yoghurt
4 bananas
100 g shredded coconut (if using
    yoghurt)
8 ice cream sticks or wooden
    skewers

SERVES 8

I. If using the chocolate, fill a saucepan a quarter full with water and bring to the boil.

2. Remove the saucepan from the element and place it carefully on a heatproof surface.

3. Break chocolate into pieces and place into a small metal bowl. Make sure the bowl is small enough to fit into the saucepan of water.

4. Using a tea towel, place your bowl of chocolate into the saucepan of water. Be careful, as the saucepan will still be hot.

5. Stir the chocolate pieces in the bowl until melted, then remove from saucepan. Make sure you use a tea towel again.

COOL TIP

Did you know that yoghurt is made by adding 'friendly' bacteria to milk and leaving it in a warm place until it becomes semi-solid. Yoghurt originally came from Turkey.

6. Cover a large plate with greaseproof paper.

7. Peel and cut the bananas in half, crosswise not lengthwise, then poke an ice cream stick into the cut end of each banana half.

8. Dip your bananas into the melted chocolate, covering half of the banana piece, then place it on the plate to set.

9. If using yoghurt instead of chocolate, sprinkle the coconut on a plate. Dip half of the banana in the yoghurt and then roll in coconut, until generously covered. Put the bananas on a plastic plate and carefully place them in the freezer for 4 or more hours.

10. Remove from freezer and eat.

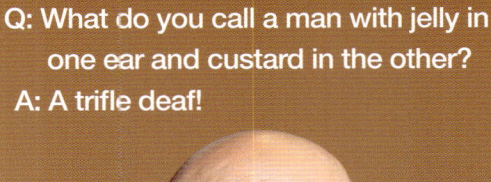

jOKE

Q: What do you call a man with jelly in one ear and custard in the other?
A: A trifle deaf!

FRUIT + YOGHURT PARFAIT

INGREDIENTS

1 cup low-fat vanilla yoghurt
2 kiwifruit, peeled and sliced
2 peaches, peeled and sliced, or
   any fruit you have at home
3 tablespoons crunchy muesli

SERVES 2

To make your parfait, layer the sliced fruit alternately with the yoghurt in clear, tall glasses. Top with crunchy muesli and serve immediately.

HANDY HINT

You can use the recipe for Nutty Muesli on page 26. You might need to use a long-handled spoon to get to all the goodies in the bottom of the glass!

FRUIT JELLY CUPS

INGREDIENTS

2 cups of fresh fruit in season, such as:
- 1 orange, peeled
- ¼ pineapple
- 1 medium kiwifruit
- 1 apple
- bunch of grapes

or you can use 2 cups of any mixture of unsweetened canned fruit

- 2 tablespoons gelatine
- juice of 1 orange
- juice of ½ lemon
- 1 tablespoon sugar
- 1 cup water

1. Chop fruit into cubes about 1-centimetre square.

2. Place gelatine into a cup or small bowl, pour over orange and lemon juice and stir with a fork until there are no lumps.

3. Sprinkle the tablespoon of sugar over the gelatine mixture.

4. Pour the gelatine mixture into a saucepan. Add the water and bring it to the boil over a medium heat, stirring all the time, until the gelatine has dissolved.

5. Once the gelatine is dissolved, remove from the heat and pour into a heatproof jug.

6. Fill 4 tall glasses with your chopped fruit, then pour the gelatine mixture into the glasses, covering the fruit.

7. Refrigerate for 2 hours or until set. Garnish with an orange wedge and a few mint leaves.

101

FRUIT KEBABS

INGREDIENTS

8–10 wooden skewers
½ cup flaked or desiccated
    coconut, toasted (optional)
⅔ cup runny honey
1 stick cinnamon or 1 teaspoon
    dried cinnamon
juice of ½ lemon
2 bananas, peeled and sliced
2 kiwifruit, peeled and sliced into
    1-centimetre rounds
2 oranges, peeled and cut into
    segments
2 apples, cored and cut into
    wedges
grapes

SERVES 6
MAKES 12 SKEWERS

1. Preheat the oven to 200°C.

2. Soak the wooden skewers by putting them in warm water for half an hour. This stops them from splitting when you thread the fruit onto them.

3. To toast the coconut, place it in a flat ovenproof dish. Put it in the preheated oven for 5–10 minutes and toast until golden brown, stirring from time to time. Watch it carefully, as it burns easily.

4. Heat the honey, cinnamon and lemon juice in a small saucepan over a low heat, or in a microwave-proof dish in the microwave, until it is hot and melted but not boiling.

5. Thread the skewers with the diced fruit. Use alternating pieces of each of the fruits until all the fruit is used and the skewers are full.

6. As you finish each kebab, place it on a large plate.

7. Brush the kebabs with the cinnamon and honey mixture, using a pastry brush, or drizzle over using a fork.

8. Roll your skewers in the toasted coconut to coat them.

MORE INGREDIENTS

Plus any 1 of the following fruit that is in season:

1 mango, peeled, stone removed and sliced

1 punnet strawberries, green tops removed

1 honeydew melon, peeled, deseeded and diced into 1–2-centimetre cubes

¡CICLE POPS

INGREDIENTS

2 cups unsweetened, fresh
  orange juice
2 tablespoons sugar
6–8 small plastic cups or popsicle
  moulds or ice cream sticks

SERVES 6-8

1. Put 1 cup of the orange juice into a small saucepan. Add the sugar and heat slowly until the sugar is dissolved. Remove from the heat.

2. Put the other cup of orange juice into a medium-sized bowl and slowly stir in the warmed juice.

3. Carefully pour into plastic cups or popsicle moulds. Put an ice cream stick into each one.

4. Place the popsicles into the freezer and leave them for at least 4 hours, or overnight, until frozen hard.

5. To remove them from their moulds, run the outside of the cup or mould under warm water until the icicle pop pops free. Enjoy!

COOL TIP

Make sure you have all the right-sized pans, baking tins and other containers needed ready before you start cooking.

CARROT CAKE

INGREDIENTS

FOR THE CAKE:

1 cup wholemeal flour
1 cup plain white flour
1¾ cups raw sugar
2 teaspoons baking soda
1 teaspoon baking powder
2 teaspoons cinnamon
¾ cup low-fat plain unsweetened
   yoghurt
1 egg
1 x 250 g can crushed
   pineapple, drained
¼ cup oil
1 cup grated carrot, firmly
   packed
¼ cup raisins (optional)
¼ cup chopped walnuts
   (optional)
1 teaspoon vanilla essence
   (optional)

SERVES 12

1. Preheat the oven to 180°C.

2. Grease a medium-sized cake tin with margarine or cooking spray.

3. In a large bowl, combine the flours, sugar, baking soda (sift this to remove the lumps), baking powder and cinnamon and mix well.

4. In a separate bowl, combine the yoghurt, egg, crushed pineapple and oil and mix well.

5. Add these wet ingredients to the dry ingredients in the large bowl and stir together to combine, until smooth.

6. Stir in the grated carrot, raisins and nuts.

7. Pour your cake batter into the prepared tin and bake for about 40 minutes in the preheated oven at 180°C until golden brown and springy to the touch.

iCiNg

CREAM CHEESE iCiNg:

½ cup light cream cheese, at room
temperature
2 tablespoons melted margarine
juice of 1 lemon
1½ cups icing sugar, sifted

8. Allow the cake to cool in the tin for about 5 minutes, then turn it out onto a wire rack. When cool to the touch the cake is ready to ice. If it is not cool, the icing will melt into the cake.

9. To make the icing, mix all the icing ingredients together in a bowl until smooth, using a food processor or whisk.

10. Spread the icing onto the cake with a butter knife or spatula.

CHOCOLATE ZUCCHINI CAKE

INGREDIENTS

3 eggs
½ cup oil
50 g melted margarine
1½ teaspoons vanilla essence
¾ cup plain unsweetened yoghurt
2 zucchini, grated
2 teaspoons orange rind, grated (optional)
2½ cups plain flour
1½ teaspoons baking soda
1½ teaspoons baking powder
½ cup cocoa
1½ cups sugar

1. Preheat oven to 180°C.

2. Grease a 20-centimetre diameter cake tin well with margarine or cooking spray. Then line the base with greaseproof paper.

3. In a large bowl, using a whisk or eggbeater, beat together the eggs, oil, melted margarine, vanilla essence and yoghurt until they are thick and frothy. Stir in the grated zucchini and orange rind.

4. Sift all the dry ingredients into a separate bowl. Add the sugar to the dry ingredients, then make a well in the middle.

5. Pour the wet ingredients into the well and stir until combined, but do not over mix, as this will make your cake 'tough'.

6. Pour the cake mixture into your prepared cake tin and bake for 40–50 minutes or until it is firm and springs back when lightly touched. Turn onto a wire rack to cool.

ICING

CHOCOLATE ICING:

2 cups icing sugar
2 tablespoons cocoa
¼ teaspoon margarine
¼ teaspoon vanilla essence
approximately 2 tablespoons very
hot water

7. To make the icing: Sift the icing sugar and cocoa into a bowl. Add the margarine and vanilla essence and mix with enough water to make a smooth, spreadable icing.

8. Spread the icing onto the cake with a butter knife or spatula.

Honey Bran Banana Muffins

Ingredients

1¾ cups self-raising flour
½ teaspoon baking soda
1¼ cups bran flakes
1 teaspoon cinnamon
1¼ cups plain unsweetened yoghurt
¼ cup runny honey
2 eggs
¼ cup oil
1 teaspoon vanilla essence (optional)
2 ripe bananas, peeled

MAKES 12

1. Preheat the oven to 180°C.

2. Grease 12 deep muffin tins, or line with paper muffin cases.

3. Sift the flour and baking soda into a large mixing bowl. Then add the bran flakes and cinnamon and mix well.

4. In a smaller bowl, beat together the yoghurt, honey, eggs, oil and vanilla essence.

5. In another bowl, mash the bananas.

6. Pour the wet ingredients into the dry ingredients. Add the mashed banana and stir everything together until just combined. Do not over mix, as this will make your muffins 'tough'.

7. Divide mixture evenly between your prepared muffin tins or cases.

8. Bake at 180°C for 20–25 minutes or until lightly browned and muffins spring back when lightly touched.

9. Let your muffins cool before sprinkling with sifted icing sugar, to serve.

If you don't have self-raising flour you can substitute 1 cup of standard flour plus one teaspoon of baking powder for each cup of self-raising flour used.

Cool Tip

TRIPLE C MUFFINS

INGREDIENTS

2 capsicums (any colour will do)
1 cup wholemeal flour
1 cup white flour
4 teaspoons baking powder
½ teaspoon salt
2 eggs
1 cup low-fat milk
50 g margarine, melted
½ cup canned corn kernels, drained
⅓ cup grated tasty cheese

MAKES 12

1. Preheat oven to 180°C.

2. Grease 12 deep muffin tins, or line with paper muffin cases.

3. Cut the capsicums in half. Remove the seeds and chop them into small pieces.

4. Sift the wholemeal and white flours, baking powder and salt into a medium-sized bowl.

5. In a separate bowl, lightly beat the eggs and milk together. Add the melted margarine, capsicum and corn and stir together until combined.

6. Pour wet mixture into the dry ingredients. Add the cheese and stir until just combined. Do not over mix, as this will make your muffins 'tough'.

7. Divide mixture evenly between your prepared muffin tins or cases.

8. Bake at 180°C for 15 minutes, or until muffins spring back when lightly touched.

THIRST QUENCHERS

BANANA TROPICANA

INGREDIENTS

1 banana, peeled and diced
1 tablespoon runny honey
½ cup low-fat milk
¼ cup low-fat coconut cream
¼ cup unsweetened pineapple
   juice, strained from crushed
   pineapple
½ cup unsweetened crushed
   pineapple
2–3 ice cubes

SERVES 2-3

1. Place all ingredients in a blender and blend until smooth.

2. Serve in tall glasses with cocktail umbrellas, or garnish with fruit slices to give that tropical feeling.

HANDY HINT

Take yourself and your friends to a magical tropical island with this great tropical drink!

BANANA-BERRY SMOOTHIE

INGREDIENTS

1. Place all your ingredients into a blender.

2. Blend until your smoothie is really smooth.

3. Serve immediately in glasses over ice.

4. Garnish with a slice of your favourite fruit.

1 cup unsweetened plain low-fat yoghurt

1 cup low-fat milk

1 cup frozen mixed berries

1 banana, peeled and cut into chunks

1 teaspoon runny honey

SERVES 3-4

HOMEMADE LEMONADE

INGREDIENTS

rind and juice of 1 lemon (you will need ⅓ cup lemon juice)
½ cup sugar
4 cups cold water

SERVES 4

1. Grate the rind off the lemon using the finest part on your grater.

2. Cut the lemon in half and squeeze the juice out using a juice squeezer.

3. Mix the lemon juice, lemon rind and sugar together in a medium-sized saucepan.

4. Add the cold water, then bring it to the boil over a medium heat. You can add a bit more lemon juice and sugar if needed at this stage, for taste.

5. Stir the mixture, then turn off the heat.

6. Let the lemonade cool, then pour it into a jug, over ice, and enjoy!

HANDY HINT

This is a real treat on hot summer days, just like in the olden days.

KIWINANA FRAPPE

INGREDIENTS

2 kiwifruit, peeled and diced
2 bananas, peeled and diced
1 cup unsweetened apple juice
1 cup crushed ice (you can buy
    this from the supermarket, or
    crush it yourself by placing
    ice cubes in a plastic bag and
    smashing with a rolling pin or
    hammer)

SERVES 3-4

1. Place all ingredients into a blender or food processor and blend until smooth.

2. Serve immediately in glasses.

MANGO LASSI

INGREDIENTS

Blend all ingredients in a blender, until smooth and creamy. Serve immediately.

1 fresh ripe mango, peeled and cubed (or you can use ½ can sliced mango, drained)
½ cup unsweetened plain yoghurt
¼ cup low-fat milk
1 cup crushed ice (see recipe for Kiwinana Frappe on opposite page)
1 teaspoon runny honey

SERVES 2

Zingy Easy Ginger Beer

Ingredients

1 teaspoon dry yeast
½ cup warm water
⅔ cup runny honey
2 tablespoons peeled and finely grated fresh ginger (or use ginger from a jar)
juice of 2 lemons, strained
4 cups hot water

Serves 4

1. Dissolve the yeast in half a cup of warm water.

2. Mix together the honey, ginger, lemon juice and the hot water in a saucepan.

3. Bring it to the boil and stir until ingredients are well combined, then pour into a clean 8-cup jar.

4. Add the yeast mixture to the jar and stir well.

5. Cover the jar with a lid, cheesecloth or clean tea towel and fasten with a large, strong rubber band.

6. Place the jar in the warm sun or hot water cupboard for 3 hours.

7. Remove the lid and use a sieve to strain your ginger beer into a jug. Refrigerate until chilled, and serve.

Cool Kids Cooking Cast

Head Chef Marco Kouch

Italian born Marco is the father of two young children. A qualified chef, Marco set up 'Cool Kids Cooking' as an after-school activity in an attempt to, in his own way, put his skills to work to help combat the unhealthy eating practices that are alarmingly commonplace in many schools and family homes in our communities. In the 'Cool Kids Cooking' series, Marco takes a comic turn as the Head Chef, the joke-telling boss of the kitchen and head taste tester.

CHEF TE KOHE TUHAKA (TK)

TK has trained as both a chef and an actor. He is passionate about food and relishes his role as mentor to his teams of 'Cool Kids Cooking' junior chefs. TK learnt to cook at an early age. He believes cooking is an essential, basic skill for all young children to have. TK's performing background includes many theatre productions and short films. He was the first actor to receive the Creative New Zealand Waka Toi Scholarship celebrating excellence among Maori practitioners in the arts. 'Cool Kids Cooking' is his first television role.

KIDS COOKING INSPECTOR JASMINE HOETJES

Jasmine is a Public Health Dietitian employed at the Auckland Regional Public Health Service. Jasmine is committed to improving the nutritional status of children and their families. Over the past year she has been implementing the Waitemata District Health Board Beverage Guidelines project in secondary schools. Jasmine's role on 'Cool Kids Cooking' is to offer interesting dietary tips and information.

Q: Why are fish poor tennis players?
A: Because they don't like to get close to the net!

Q: What do you get if you put three ducks in a box?
A: A box of quackers!

Q: What did the mayonnaise say to the refrigerator?
A: Close the door, I'm dressing!

Q: What has bread on both sides and is scared of everything?
A: A chicken sandwich!

Q: How do you fix a broken pumpkin?
A: With a pumpkin patch!

Q: What did the orange say to the doctor?
A: I'm not peeling very well.

Q: How do you fix a broken tomato?
A: With tomato paste!

Q: Why did the chicken want to join the band?
A: So that he could practise using his drumsticks!

Q: What did baby corn say to Mama corn?
A: Where's Pop-corn?!

Q: What did the raspberry say to the blueberry?
A: I love you berry, berry much!

Q: Why is history like a fruitcake?
A: Because it's full of dates!

Q: Why did the tomato turn green?
A: Because it saw the salad dressing!

Q: Why did the orange go to the petrol station?
A: Because it ran out of juice!

Q: What did the girl mushroom say to the boy mushroom?
A: You look like a fungi!

WHERE DID 5+ A DAY COME FROM?

United Fresh NZ Inc. was formed in 1991 to bring all the New Zealand growers of fresh fruit and vegetables together. The idea was to help people be healthier by encouraging them to eat more fresh fruit and vegetables. This is where 5+ A Day came in.

5+ A DAY

Launched in 1994, the 5+ A Day programme started as a one-day event in primary schools thoughout the country.

The programme has grown to include both primary schools and early childhood education centres nationwide. In the month of November 2006, this involved around 400,000 children.

5+ A Day, The Colour Way Facts

- 5+ A Day = 5 or more servings of fresh fruit and vegetables every day.

- Ideally 3 servings of vegetables and 2 servings of fruit.

- 5 is the minimum (that is why they have the + in their logo).

- A serving is about a handful (this is why they have the hand in their logo).

- We all use our own hands to measure our own servings therefore a serving for a child is smaller than a serving for an adult.

The Colour Way

- There are five colour groups in the colour way — red, yellow/orange, brown/white, green and blue/purple.

- By eating your colours you can help to keep yourself healthy.

- Colourful fruit and vegetables contain many vitamins, minerals and phytochemicals (fight-o-chemicals) your body needs to maintain good health and energy.

- Many of the phytochemicals give the fruit and vegetables their colour.

INDEX

INDEX
CONTINUED

iNDEX
CONTiNUED

INGREDIENTS

135

YOUR RECIPE

....

INGREDIENTS